Favorite Things Old and New

How do things get to be favorites?

page 14

READING ACROSS TEXTS

page 16

Keepsakes

by Leland B. Jacobs

I keep bottle caps,
    I keep strings,
I keep keys and corks
    And all such things.

When people say,
"What good are they?"
The answer's hard to get
For just how I will use them all
I don't know yet.

Favorite Times

People often save keepsakes from special times in their lives. Think of something that you do with family or friends. Does it happen each week, each month, or even once a year? This is called a tradition. Make a keepsake box about a tradition.

Collect Facts and Ideas

1 Choose a tradition you share with family or friends. Find pictures or things that tell about this tradition. These things are called keepsakes.

2 Ask your family or friends to tell what they like about this tradition. Find out how it got started.

Put It All Together

3 Make a chart like this one. Write the questions below. Draw pictures to answer the questions.
  • What do I do on this day?
  • What do I like best about this day?
  • What do others like about this day?

Prepare and Share

4 Cut out each group of pictures. Write about each group. Put your pictures, writings, and keepsakes together in a box. Make a cover for your box. Share your keepsake box with your class.

What Kind of Baby-sitter Is This?

written and illustrated by Dolores Johnson

Kevin's mother was getting all dressed up to go out. And then the doorbell rang.

"Not another baby-sitter!" cried Kevin. "You said you'd take me with you next time! If you leave tonight I . . . I . . . I . . . I'm not going to be your friend!"

"Kevin," said his mother. "This is Mrs. Lovey Pritchard. She'll take care of you while I'm away at school."

"Take a look at that face, that sweet little face," said the baby-sitter. "You can call me Aunt Lovey, sugar dumpling."

"Mom, take me with you!" yelled Kevin.

"So you're the little boy who doesn't like baby-sitters," said Aunt Lovey. Well, we're going to have such fun together."

"Mom, don't leave me with her, puullleeeeease!" yelled Kevin.

"Don't worry about us, little mother," said the baby-sitter. "Kevin and I will be just fine."

"Well, I'm leaving, too!" said Kevin as he stormed through the kitchen out to the back porch. "That old lady will never miss me. She'll be busy doing what baby-sitters do—painting her toenails, talking on the telephone, and eating the good stuff in the refrigerator. Hey, she'd better not eat that last piece of cake!"

Kevin sneaked back into the kitchen. "Isn't she even gonna come after me? Is that lady so dumb she doesn't even know I'm gone?"

From his hiding place, Kevin heard the click of a switch and then the roar of the television. "So that's what she's doing. She's watching soap operas. And my mom is paying her a zillion dollars to watch *me*."

Aunt Lovey started yelling, jumping up and down, and clapping. "She's watching my baseball game! My *mom* wouldn't even watch it. What kind of baby-sitter is this? She's supposed to be yelling at *me*."

The baby-sitter started pulling things from her handbag. She put a baseball cap on her head. She laid some baseball cards on the couch, and she waved a pennant in the air.

"I wish she would put that pennant down," said Kevin. "I can hardly see."

"And it's a Badger pennant," continued Kevin. "That proves it. She doesn't know anything about baseball. Everybody knows that the Badgers can't win."

When the ball game ended, and the Badgers had won, Aunt Lovey turned off the television set. She was so busy pulling things out of her purse, it seems she never even noticed Kevin.

"Oh, no," said Kevin. "Here it comes now . . . her telephone numbers . . . her nail polish . . . those kissy-kissy books that baby-sitters read."

But Aunt Lovey pulled out a book about baseball, opened it, and began to read softly.

"I wish she would speak up," said Kevin. "I can hardly hear."

So Kevin crawled closer and Aunt Lovey read louder, and they read, and played games, and told jokes, and laughed so much that they didn't even notice when Kevin's mother came home.

"Are you still angry with me, sweetheart?" Kevin's mother asked when she came in. "I really hated to leave you. But, of course, there'll be other times when I'll have to go out."

"Well, that's all right, Mom, 'cause I've got a great idea," said Kevin. "Can Aunt Lovey move in with us? We can make her a bed on the couch, or she can share your bedroom with you. This can be her home, too."

"But, Kevin," said his mother, "Aunt Lovey has her own home. Baby-sitters don't stay over."

"Mom, you don't understand. Aunt Lovey's no baby-sitter—she's my friend!"

Dolores Johnson

Dolores Johnson remembers her own problems with baby-sitters when she was a girl. That is why she wrote *What Kind of Baby-sitter Is This?*. Her other stories are about solving problems too.

Dolores Johnson also draws the pictures for her stories. She thinks writing books for children is fun. Ms. Johnson hopes boys and girls think her stories are fun to read too!

Read More and Share

Here are three more stories by Dolores Johnson.

My Mom Is My Show-and-Tell

The Best Bug to Be

What Will Mommy Do When I'm at School?

Pretend you are a child from one of Dolores Johnson's stories. Introduce yourself to your class. Tell your class the story as if it happened to you.

Let's Play Ball

Kevin and his baby-sitter love baseball. Do you know how baseball got started?

The idea for baseball came from an old game called rounders. In that game, the feeder (pitcher) threw a small ball, and the striker (batter) hit the ball with a stick. Home base was a rock called the castle.

The first real baseball team was called the Knickerbockers. The team changed the rules and called their new game baseball. Soon everyone was playing the game. Baseball became a favorite American game!

Baseball cards have been around for a very long time. The first set was made over 100 years ago!

The President of the United States throws out the first pitch of the first game of the season!

During the seventh inning of a baseball game, it is tradition for fans in the stadium to stand up and "stretch" before their team bats. Fans sometimes sing "Take Me Out to the Ball Game."

Check It Out

Find a newspaper. What sports are listed in the sports section? Look for *statistics*. Statistics, or stats, tell how players and their teams are doing. Look at sport magazines. How is the magazine different from the newspaper? Cut out pictures of sporting events from newspapers and magazines. Glue the pictures on a large piece of paper to make a sports poster.

Mei-Mei Loves the Morning

by Margaret Holloway Tsubakiyama
illustrated by Cornelius Van Wright and Ying-Hwa Hu

MEI-MEI loves the morning. When she
wakes up, she always hears Bai-Ling rustling
impatiently in his cage and Grandpa's
slippers slip-slapping on the kitchen floor.
Mother and Father are still asleep, but Mei-
Mei jumps out of bed.

Mei-Mei loves the morning because
Grandpa lets her unzip the night cover on
Bai-Ling's cage. Mei-Mei looks inside the
cage. Bai-Ling's eyes are shining in the
darkness. When Mei-Mei lifts off the cover,
Bai-Ling begins to sing.

Mei-Mei fills a tiny bowl with millet and another with water for Bai-Ling's breakfast. Grandpa fills bowls with rice porridge for Mei-Mei and himself. Mei-Mei puts pickled vegetables on hers. They are so sour that her mouth puckers when she eats them.

After breakfast they put on their coats and go down to the lobby where Grandpa keeps his bicycle. Grandpa gives Bai-Ling's cage to Mei-Mei. It is so heavy that she needs both hands to hang it on the handlebars.

Slowly, slowly, they ride down the block. Mei-Mei sits at the front of the bicycle. A cool wind blows, but it's warm in Grandpa's arms.

Even though it is still early, the street is busy. The peddlers are setting up their stalls, waiting for the first customers of the day. Everyone is in a hurry. Only the farmers are still asleep, snoring in their trucks full of potatoes and cabbage. "Wake up, sleepyheads!" calls a man as he rides by. "It's morning!"

At the corner Grandpa stops to talk with the cobbler. Mei-Mei watches the cobbler tap on a lady's red shoe with his tiny hammer. He polishes the shoe with a soft cloth until it shines like a lacquer bowl.

Grandpa lifts Mei-Mei off the bicycle. The cobbler lets her try the shoes on. Grandpa smiles when Mei-Mei walks like a princess in the beautiful red shoes.

Down the street they ride, through the round moon gate, and into the park. Grandpa hugs Mei-Mei to make sure she doesn't fall as they go over the bump.

In the park their friends are waiting at their favorite bench beneath the plum tree. They have saved a place for Mei-Mei and Grandpa on the bench and one for Bai-Ling in the tree.

Grandpa lifts Mei-Mei up to hand Bai-Ling's cage on a branch. The whole tree is filled with songbirds, and the whole tree is singing.

They stay at the park all morning long.
Mei-Mei and her friend Xiao-Chen do tai-chi
with Grandpa. They pretend to tame a tiger
and to grab a bird by the feathers of its tail.
They pretend they are carrying big balls in
their hands. Everyone moves slowly and
carefully. Then they stop, still as white
cranes in the grass.

   After they exercise Grandpa gives Mei-
Mei a jar of tea. The warm jar feels good
in her hands. Grandpa and his friends swirl
their tea and drink and talk. Mei-Mei and
Xiao-Chen just swirl theirs and watch the
tea leaves all fall down.

The sun is already hot when they leave the park. Grandpa puts his cap on Mei-Mei's head. His cap is so big that from under its brim Mei-Mei can barely see all the bicycles. Some carry vegetables to market; others bring students to school. One bicycle is even piled high with mattresses.

Mei-Mei sees a pig poking its head from a basket. The pig squeals angrily as the bicycle rides by. Mei-Mei snuggles deep into Grandpa's arms.

They stop at the corner. The lao-bing man's stove is hot, and his pancakes sizzle.

"How many today?" he asks. Mei-Mei holds up four fingers. The lao-bing man wraps four crisp pancakes in a sheet of newspaper and hands them to her. Mei-Mei holds them in her pocket, warm all the way home.

Grandpa parks his bicycle in the lobby.
Mei-Mei jumps off the bicycle into his arms.

"I love the morning, Grandpa," says Mei-Mei.

Grandpa hugs her tight. "I love it, too," he says.

A Special Day

Mei-Mei spends each morning with her grandpa. This is a special time for her. People write about special times in a diary. You can write about a special time. Pretend you are writing in your own diary. Tell about a very special day in your life.

- What happened that day?
- How did you feel?
- What do you remember most about that day? Read what you wrote to your friends.

What do they think about your special day?

Explore with

Mei-Mei rides a bicycle. A bicycle is a machine. A machine makes work easier. The wheels on a bicycle help you move.

A simple machine is a tool with few or no moving parts. A wheel is a simple machine. There are six kinds of simple machines.

Lever
Levers help you move objects.

Screw
Screws hold things together.

Wedge
Wedges push or split things apart.

Inclined plane
Inclined planes help move things to a higher or lower place.

Pulley
Pulleys move things up, down, or sideways.

Wheel and axle
A wheel and axle moves or turns things.

Simple Machines

Be an Inventor!

Look around for simple machines. Think about how they work. Then make your own machine.

What You Need

books about machines
rulers and other flat surfaces
boxes, blocks, spools, screws,
string, rope, rubber bands, wheels

What You Do

1 Look at your materials. Think about different ways to put them together.

2 Make a machine that can roll, push, pull, or lift other things.

3 Name your machine.

Use What You Learn

4 Share your machine with the class. Tell what the machine does. Why is it important?

Reader Response

Think About a Question

1 How do things get to be favorites? Think about why Kevin liked his baby-sitter. Think about why Mei-Mei liked the morning. Think about why you like your favorite things. Write about your ideas.

Ask a Question

2 Pretend you are visiting Mei-Mei in China. Write questions you would ask her about her special mornings.

Use New Words

3 Look for new words in *Mei-Mei Loves the Morning*. Write the words on note cards. On different note cards, write what each word means. Mix up the cards. Match each word with the card that tells what it means.

Connect What You Read

4 How are Mei-Mei and Kevin alike? How are they different? Write about your ideas.

Take a Careful Look

5 Think about the people in both stories. Why do you think Mei-Mei loved being with her grandpa so much? Why do you think Kevin liked his baby-sitter? Write your answer.